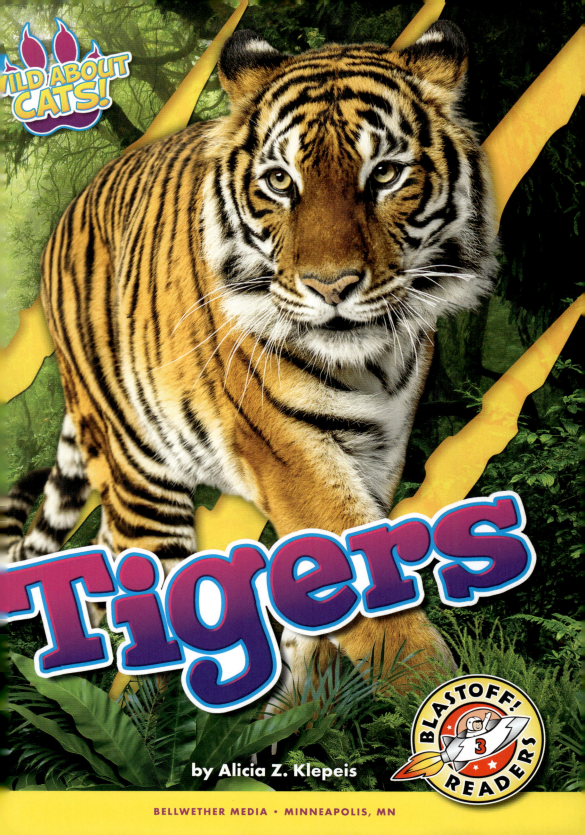

Blastoff! Readers are carefully developed by literacy experts to build reading stamina and move students toward fluency by combining standards-based content with developmentally appropriate text.

Level 1 provides the most support through repetition of high-frequency words, light text, predictable sentence patterns, and strong visual support.

Level 2 offers early readers a bit more challenge through varied sentences, increased text load, and text-supportive special features.

Level 3 advances early-fluent readers toward fluency through increased text load, less reliance on photos, advancing concepts, longer sentences, and more complex special features.

★ **Blastoff! Universe**

Reading Level — Grade K → Grades 1–3 → Grade 4

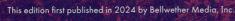

This edition first published in 2024 by Bellwether Media, Inc.

No part of this publication may be reproduced in whole or in part without written permission of the publisher. For information regarding permission, write to Bellwether Media, Inc., Attention: Permissions Department, 6012 Blue Circle Drive, Minnetonka, MN 55343.

Library of Congress Cataloging-in-Publication Data

LC record for Tigers available at: https://lccn.loc.gov/2023046590

Text copyright © 2024 by Bellwether Media, Inc. BLASTOFF! READERS and associated logos are trademarks and/or registered trademarks of Bellwether Media, Inc.

Editor: Betsy Rathburn   Designer: Brittany McIntosh

Printed in the United States of America, North Mankato, MN.

Table of Contents

Cool Coats   4
Claws For Climbing   8
Ambush Hunters   12
Watch and Learn   18
Glossary   22
To Learn More   23
Index   24

Cool Coats

Tigers are the world's biggest cat **species**. They are known for their striped coats. No two coats are the same!

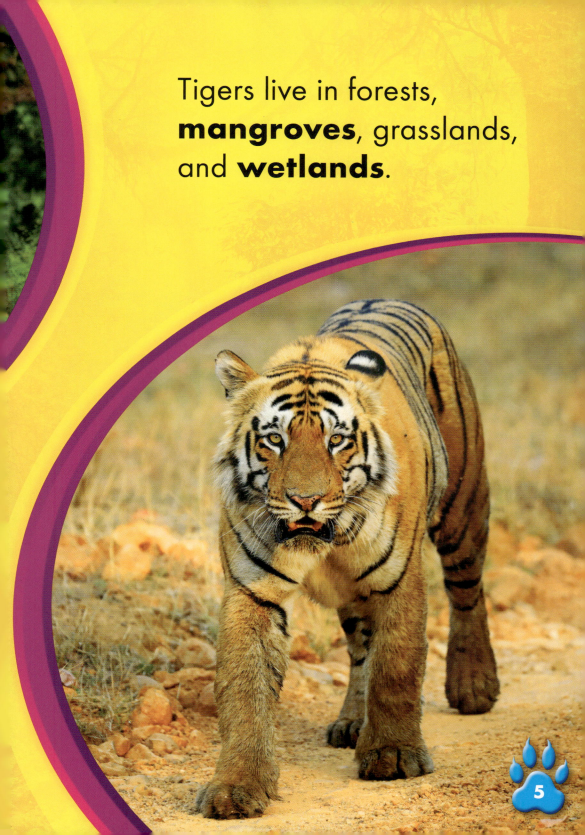

Tigers live in forests, **mangroves**, grasslands, and **wetlands**.

All wild tigers live in Asia. India is home to more tigers than any other country.

Tigers are **endangered**. Their numbers are going down. Hunting and **habitat** loss are the main causes.

Claws For Climbing

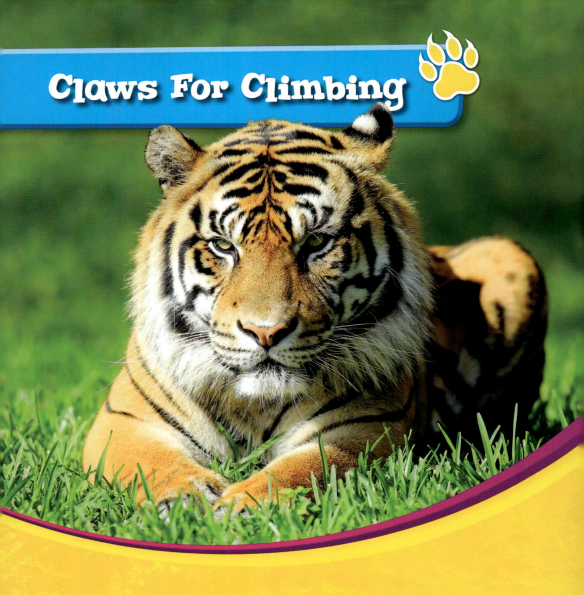

Tigers usually have orange coats with black stripes. They have white stomachs and white markings on their ears and faces.

Partially **webbed** toes help tigers swim. Sharp claws help them climb and scratch trees.

Identify a Tiger

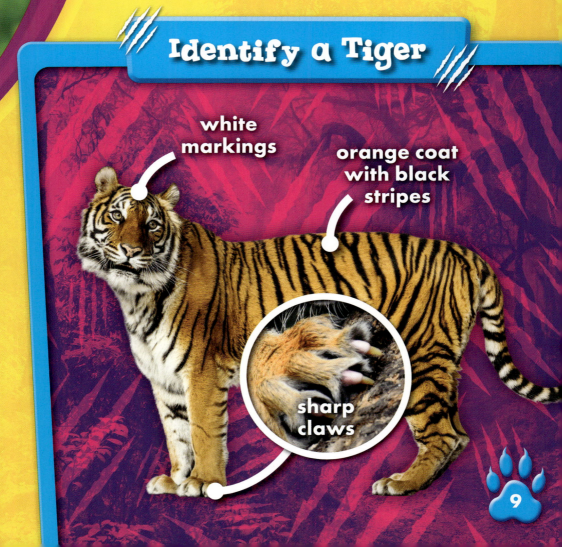

white markings

orange coat with black stripes

sharp claws

The biggest tigers are over 10 feet (3 meters) long!

Male tigers are bigger than females. The heaviest males may weigh over 600 pounds (272 kilograms).

Ambush Hunters

Tigers mainly hunt at night. Excellent eyesight helps them find **prey** in the dark.

These **ambush** hunters usually hunt on their own. They follow their prey quietly. When they get close enough, they **pounce**!

Tigers are **carnivores**. They eat deer and wild boar. Monkeys and fish are also common foods.

Tigers can eat over 80 pounds (36 kilograms) of food in one sitting! They save some of their food to eat later.

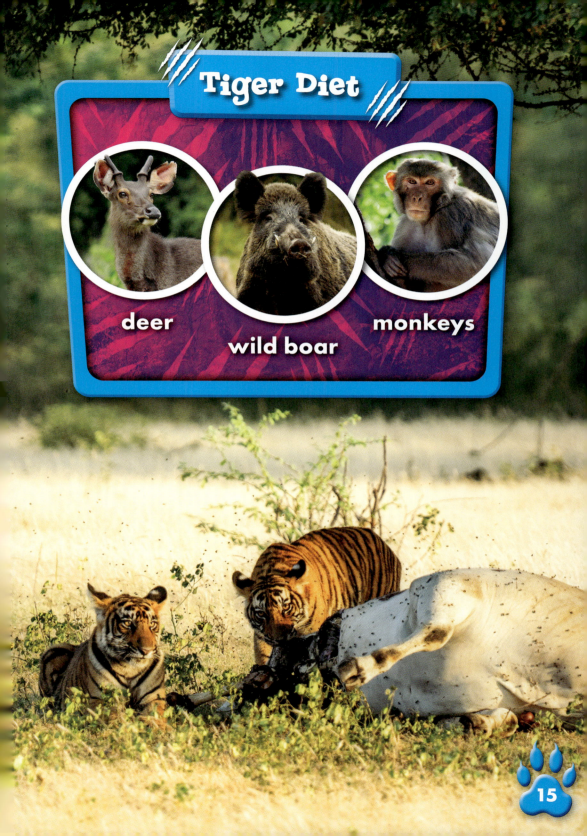

Tigers are usually **solitary**. Females with babies keep their cubs close.

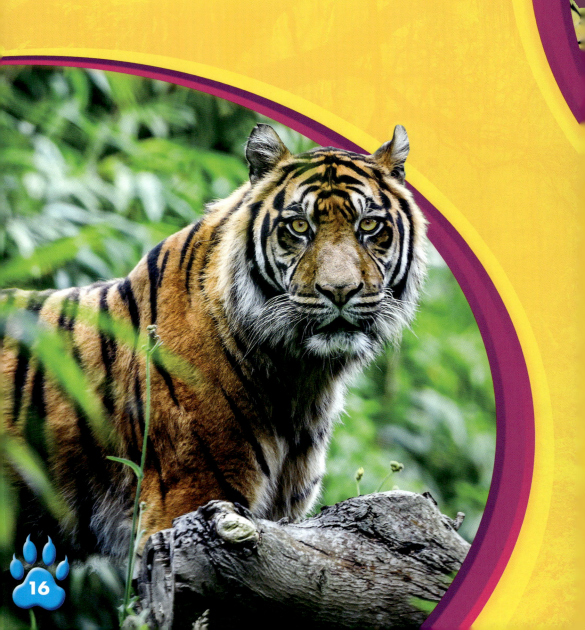

Tigers scratch and pee on trees to mark their **territory**. These signs tell other tigers to go away!

Watch and Learn

Females give birth in **dens**. These can be in caves, hollow trees, or thick grass. **Litters** usually have two to four cubs.

Cubs chase and tackle each other. They practice ambushing their mom while she rests!

Baby Tigers

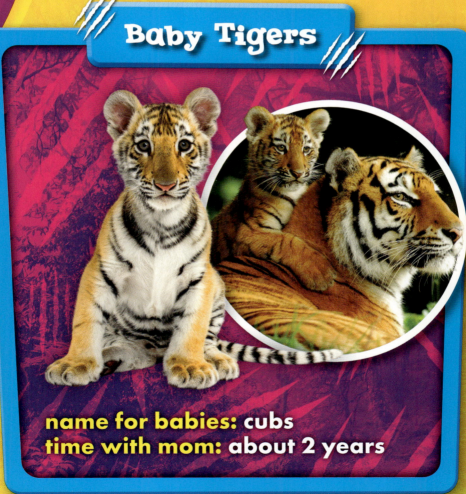

name for babies: cubs
time with mom: about 2 years

Cubs leave the den at around two months old. They learn to hunt by watching mom. In a few months, they hunt with her.

Cubs are on their own in about two years. They can roam free!

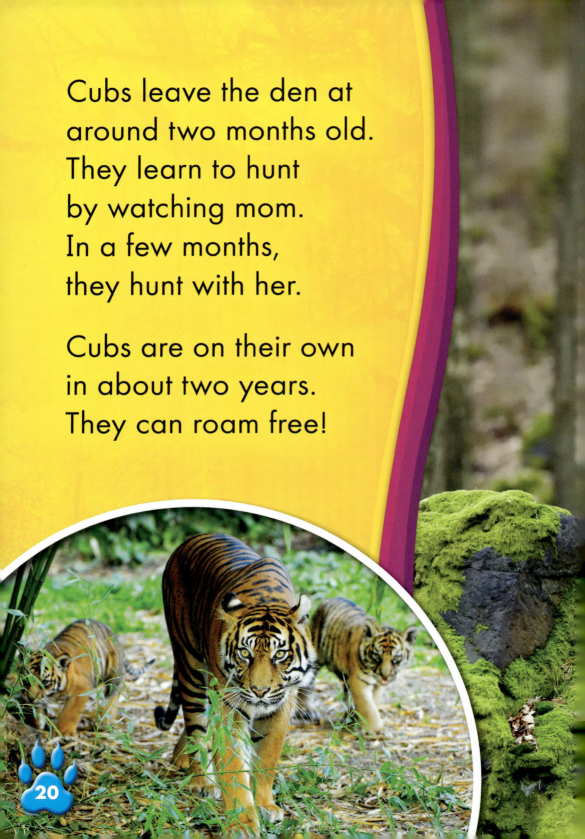

In the Wild

habitats:

forests mangroves grasslands wetlands

conservation status: endangered

Least Concern | Near Threatened | Vulnerable | Endangered | Critically Endangered | Extinct in the Wild | Extinct

population in the wild: fewer than 5,600
population trend: going down
life span: up to 18 years

Glossary

ambush—an attack from a hiding place

carnivores—animals that only eat meat

dens—sheltered places

endangered—at risk of dying out

habitat—a land area with certain types of plants, animals, and weather

litters—groups of babies that are born at the same time

mangroves—groups of trees and shrubs that grow along coastlines

pounce—to suddenly jump on something

prey—animals that are hunted by other animals for food

solitary—living alone

species—kinds of animals

territory—the land area where an animal lives

webbed—having an area of skin between the fingers or toes

wetlands—lands that are covered with low levels of water for most of the year

To Learn More

AT THE LIBRARY

Downs, Kieran. *Asiatic Lion vs. Bengal Tiger*. Minneapolis, Minn.: Bellwether Media, 2023.

Feldman, Thea. *Tigers Can't Purr! And Other Amazing Facts*. New York, N.Y.: Simon & Schuster, 2020.

Mills, Andrea. *Big Cats*. New York, N.Y.: DK Publishing, 2019.

ON THE WEB

FACTSURFER

Factsurfer.com gives you a safe, fun way to find more information.

1. Go to www.factsurfer.com.

2. Enter "tigers" into the search box and click 🔍.

3. Select your book cover to see a list of related content.

Index

ambush hunters, 13
Asia, 6
carnivores, 14
claws, 9
coats, 4, 8
colors, 8
cubs, 16, 18, 19, 20
dens, 18, 20
endangered, 7
eyesight, 12
females, 11, 16, 18, 19, 20
food, 14, 15
forests, 5
grasslands, 5
habitat loss, 7
hunting, 7, 12, 13, 20
identify, 9
in the wild, 21
India, 6
litters, 18
males, 11
mangroves, 5

markings, 8
numbers, 7
pounce, 13
prey, 12, 13, 14, 15
range, 6, 7
scratch, 9, 17
size, 4, 10, 11
size comparison, 11
solitary, 16
stripes, 4, 8
swim, 9
territory, 17
webbed toes, 9
wetlands, 5

The images in this book are reproduced through the courtesy of: Eric Isselee, front cover (tiger), pp. 3, 9 (tiger), 11 (tiger), 19 (cub); Teo Tarras, front cover (background); imageBROKER.com GmbH & Co. KG/ Alamy, pp. 4, 19 (inset), 20; Kit Day/ Alamy, p. 5; Rajat Bhandari/ Alamy, p. 6; Imagebroker/ Alamy, p. 8; Suntisook.D, p. 9 (inset); Martin Mecnarowski, pp. 10-11; Nynke van Holten, p. 11 (house cat); Zocha_K, p. 12; Nature Picture Library/ Alamy, p. 13; Ewa Studio, p. 14; Sourabh Bharti, pp. 14-15; Yhamdeestudios, p. 15 (deer); WildMedia, p. 15 (wild boar); Storm Is Me, p. 15 (monkeys); Hung Chung Chih, p. 16; lumen-digital, p. 17; slowmotiongli, p. 18; Karel Bartik, pp. 20-21; ehtesham, p. 23.